SEVEN
ANGLO-SAXON
ELEGIES

FACSIMILE OF A PAGE FROM THE EXETER BOOK.

4

SEVEN ANGLO-SAXON ELEGIES

from the
EXETER BOOK
transcribed and
translated by

Louis Rodrigues

with six illustrations
by **Jo Nathan**
and one (p.79) from
the Junius manuscript.

6

PREFACE

So profound was the impression made upon my sensibilities by a reading of **The Wanderer** by one of my first professors of Anglo-Saxon, Gavin Cochrane Martin, as far back as 1958, that the compulsion to capture in a Modern English rendering the spirit in which that poem was composed by its anonymous author has haunted me ever since. Even after twenty-five drafts spanning almost as many years, I find myself correcting and re-correcting what I had once considered as final. Such is the nature of Anglo-Saxon verse and so much has the language lost in the interim that the end product will continue to demonstrate the pitiful inadequacy of Modern English to duplicate the essential qualities of its original: its rhythms, its imagery, its lexis, its style.

Strangely enough, the other poems occasioned less difficulty and, consequently, less dissatisfaction in their rendering; and the one that I am most pleased with is **The Ruin**. Of **The Husband's Message** I have written at greater length in a doctoral thesis on *Anglo-Saxon Verse Runes*; and, any lover of Anglo-Saxon verse may wish to explore the whole fascinating subject of runes in this critical edition that is provided with a glossary and twenty-five plates.

L.J.R., Cambridge, 1991.

8

CONTENTS

10

Introduction

There is a small group of poems in the Exeter
Book to which the term 'elegies' is given: **The
Wanderer, The Seafarer, Deor, Wulf and Eadwacer,
The Wife's Lament, The Husband's Message** and
The Ruin. These titles, invented by Benjamin
Thorpe in 1836, have remained unchanged to the
present day. Not all editors would agree, however, to restricting the number to seven since at
least eight or nine more (notably **The Rhyming
Poem, Resignation A** and **Resignation B)** are felt
to exemplify the *genre.* Besides these complete
poems in the Exeter Book, C. L. Wrenn(1) cites
parts of others as being elegiac in tone, such as
lines 2444-2462 and 2247-2266 in **Beowulf** (one,
the lament of a father for a son who has ended
on the gallows, the other, the lament of the last
survivor of a glorious race); the Epilogue to
Cynewulf's **Elene**; and, the poet's individual ut-
terances at the close of **The Dream of the Rood.**

Greenfield and Calder(2) maintain that, although
the group is labelled *elegies,* they conform neither
to the classical concept of being "composed in a
specific meter" nor to the post-Renaissance one
of being "lamentations for the loss of specific
persons or communities;" that, in fact, they are
"a heterogeneous lot" since different *genres* have
been proposed for them singly or as parts of
small groups." To a certain extent this is true.
The Ruin might be seen as an *encomium urbis;*
The Wanderer as a *consolatio,* together with **The
Seafarer** as a *planctus,* or together with the latter
and **Resignation** as a penitential poem; **Wulf and
Eadwacer** as a riddle. **The Wanderer, The Seafarer,** and **The Rhyming Poem** might each be seen

12

as homiletic; The Wife's Lament, The Husband's Message, and Wulf and Eadwacer as love-poems. Whatever their ultimate sub-classification, Wrenn (3) sees the recurrent theme of this group as "the grief of exile, whether from native land or for the earthly pilgrim for the heavenly home ..... the remembering of vanished past joys and glories and the feeling of present desolation made endurable for the Christian poet only by thoughts of celestial happiness." T. A. Shippey(4) describes all seven as "urgent and passionate poems."

The Ruin, as we now have it, consists of 49 lines and follows immediately upon The Husband's Message in the Exeter Book. Lines 12-18 and the eight after 41, like so many of the Riddles, were damaged by the same destructive agent. Incomplete as it is, the poem is clearly elegiac in its lament for the loss of ancient glories and its consciousness of present decay. Unlike the others in the group, the utterance is not a personal one. It is that of the poet throughout.

The poet is gazing on the ruins of a city believed to be *Aquae Sulis* (Bath), described as *enta geweorc* ('the work of giants') like the similar ruin of The Wanderer 87, *eald enta geweorc* ('the ancient work of giants'). He meditates on this scene of crumbling decay, contrasting its present devastation with its past beauty. Either war or pestilence has destroyed its builders and rulers; but, it was once a fair city with its numerous bathhouses and its halls filled with revelry. The elegiac meditation is general, and there is nothing of the sort of moralizing and Christian piety of The Wanderer or The Seafarer in it. The cause of the desolation here is *wyrd* ('fate') not God.

In its accumulation of closely focussed detail, its
powerful rhetoric with its internal rhymes, its
unique vocabulary, its compressed and separate
images that describe the decaying present as op-
posed to its sweeping syntactic movement that
evokes the glories of the past, The Ruin is re-
markable for its ability to convey, even in its
brief and fragmentary state, some genuine poetic
feeling.

The Wanderer, 115 lines long, is the finest of all
the elegies. Despite its complex construction,
which has provoked considerable critical contro-
versy, the poem demonstrates a clear sequence
of thought, with a definite beginning and end. To
this extent it is complete and convincing as a
whole. The three *topoi* that it encompasses -
the exile theme, the ruin theme, and the *ubi sunt*
motif - occupy lines 8-110. This central section
of the poem is considered to be the utterance of
a homeless exile or wanderer, a *thegn* who has
lost his lord and kinsmen. It is preceded by a
prologue of five lines in which the poet comments
on the fate and prospects of exile and two further
lines that introduce the protagonist. The epilogue
that follows this section consists also of five lines,
but of the lengthened type called 'hypermetric,'
occasionally used for stylistic effects.

The first part of the *eardstapa's* ('earth-stepper's')
monologue (8-63) treats of the theme of exile -
of the loss of his gold-giver and his companions,
the erstwhile joys of the mead-hall, his search
for a new lord, and the physical and mental hardships he has suffered. As he rows across the
sea, he falls into a reverie in which his former
comrades appear vividly before him once again,

only to make his lonely misery the more poignant when they depart as silently as they came. Meditating on his own trials, he begins to reflect on how the sudden departure of his former comrades from the banquet-hall of life reminds him of the general misery of the world.

The nine lines (64-72) of homiletic moralizing that follow serve as a link between the earlier theme of exile and the later theme of ruin. This latter theme, which forms the second part of the monologue (73-84), begins with reflections on the imminent end of the world and develops into a meditation on universal transitoriness as the 'wanderer' contemplates the ruins of what was once a stone-built Roman citadel.

In the third part of the monologue (92-110), there occur the most famous lines of the poem that emphasize the *ubi sunt* motif in a series of rhetorical questions that vividly recall the vanished glories of the past (92-3).

The close of the poem echoes its beginning with a gnomic-homiletic exhortation to seek true security with the Father in heaven.

The Seafarer, 124 lines long, is usually linked with **The Wanderer** with which it shares a similarity in tone and poetic quality. Unlike **The Wanderer**, however, whose monologue is tied to an authorial voice at beginning and end, this poem, like the other elegies, employs the fictitious "I." It is also more specifically Christian. The poem's first 102 lines are generally considered to constitute the whole piece - the last 21 lines, gnomic-holmiletic, and of a more inferior quality to the rest, an addition.

Lines 1-102 divide into two parts: the first (1-64a)
treats of the narrator's hardships at sea; the
second (64b-102) is mainly homiletic and parallels
The Wanderer in many respects. The first part
begins with the seafarer's remembrance of past
sufferings on the sea - its terrors, its loneliness,
its desolation - which, in comparison with its
excitements, fail to deter him from setting out
on yet another voyage. It is a vivid and moving
description of sea-voyaging presented in a lively
dramatic form suggestive more of a dialogue of
inner voices than of an interior monologue. In
contrast to the 'wanderer,' who twice invokes "he
who knows," he who has experienced similar sorrow and loss (29, 37), the 'seafarer' thrice con-
trasts his lot with that of the prosperous man on
land, one who does not know how the narrator
had to dwell in exile or what he suffered there
(12, 29, 55-7). He reinforces his sense of desolation and isolation by references to seabirds as
his only companions and source of joy (19-26).
After the second allusion to the land-dweller who
cannot believe what he has endured, and a description of the earth fettered by darkness, snow,
frost and hail (29-33), he says that it is for this
that his spirit urges him to a sea-journey, to
seek an alien land (33-8). An impersonal passage
(39-47) now follows, expressing every man's (and
by implication the speaker's) fears about the out-
come of a sea-journey. But the blossoming world
and the sad-voiced cuckoo (summer's herald) urge
on the one who thinks of travelling far upon the
sea-ways (48-56). The second part, beginning at
64b, is essentially eschatologoical in nature: first,
the admission of the inevitability of death (66b-
71); then a recommendation of the value of leav-
ing for posterity a glorious memory through noble

deeds and warfare against the devil in this life
(72-80a); then a comment on the decline of
earthly splendour (80b-90); finally, a graphic description of old age, an observation on the vanity
of mortal things, a reminder that gold cannot
help the sinful soul, that God's power is terrible
and real, and that death comes unexpectedly (91-
102).

The last 21 lines (103-24) are decidedly inferior in
quality to the rest of the poem and are of the
gnomic versifying kind which seems to have been
commonplace in Anglo-Saxon poetry.

Deor, a 42-line poem, is divided in the Exeter
Book, into groups of between three and eight
lines, marked off as stanzaic by the use of initial
capitals, and each, except the sixth (28-35), con-
cluded with an identical line, commonly regarded
as a refrain. The sixth and seventh stanzas are
not separated in the manuscript by the otherwise
regular special sign placed at the end of each
group-refrain. This has led to the belief that the
sixth group is an interpolation, for the reason
that its homiletic tone does not accord with the
rest of the poem. However, as Wrenn points out,
such homiletic moralizing is not inappropriate in
an Anglo-Saxon poem; nor, to an Anglo-Saxon
audience, would its Christian tone seem incon-
sistent with the traditional matter of the rest of
the poem.

In this, "the most perfect of Old English poems
on a small scale"(6), the first five stanzas allude
specifically to characters from Germanic legend
and history connected with situations of difficulty: *Welund, Beadohild, Maethhild, Theodric* and

Eormanric. The sixth is a gnomic reflection on the wise Lord's granting of mercy to some and a portion of woes to others. The seventh provides the fictitious elegiac framework for the whole poem.

The *scop* Deor (whose name is probably symbolic) cites *Welund's* captivity by *Nithhad, Beadohild's* rape by the smith in revenge for her father's barbarous cruelty towards him, *Maethhild's* sorrowful love, *Theodric's* exile, and *Eormanric's* tyranny, as examples of trials successfully borne and from which he can draw consolation for his own - his displacement in his lord's favour by *Heorrenda.* The use of the refrain, "That passed away; so may this," with the meaning, in the earlier stanzas, of "that grief passed; so can this one," acquires a twist in the final stanza, for "that" refers to Deor's former *prosperity,* now passed away as completely as ancient grief.

Wulf and Eadwacer, a 19-line fragment that follows **Deor** in the Exeter Book, was once known as 'The First Riddle' because of its enigmatic quality and because it immediately precedes the first group of **Riddles.** It derives its title from the names of its two characters: Wulf, believed by some critics to be an outlaw and the speaker's lover, and Eadwacer, the detested husband. Others have taken Wulf to be the outlawed husband and Eadwacer her gaoler, who has forced his attentions upon her. The "whelp," according to the first theory, is the husband's child, which Wulf is carrying away to the forest; according to the second, Wulf's. The story probably derives from some lost Germanic tradition; and, like **The Wife's Lament,** may well be a survival of Germanic folk-

18

songs once sung by women, as Kemp Malone(7)
suggests. Certainly, the simplicity of its very
direct language and the musical element in its
verse, together with the refrain, reminiscent of
Deor, would support this view.

The lady and Wulf are on separate islands, kept
apart by the cruel Eadwacer. Either the lady's
own poeple or even the fierce inhabitants of
Wulf's desolate island might have received him;
but they can never come together. She sits in
tears and misery, forced to endure the embraces
of Eadwacer which are both pleasurable and
loathsome to her. It is doubting thoughts of her
love, not hunger, that make her miserable. Wulf
will carry off their wretched offspring to the
forest.

The poem's appeal seems to lie in its obscurity -
its thematic patterning, its style: in the refrain,
in the pathetic fallacy of rainy weather and
weeping; in the shifts in syntax and line lengths;
in its unmetrical and plaintive *Wulf min Wulf*(13).
Allusive and incomplete as the poem is, it is the
most passionate of love lyrics that has survived
in Anglo-Saxon.

The Husband's Message is generally considered to
be 53 lines long and not to include the group of
17 lines, commonly referred to as **Riddle 60**, that
precede it in the manuscript. The three sectional
divisions of **The Husband's Message,** however, in
their initial capitalization and complete resem-
blance in form to **Riddle 60**, have led some
editors to designate the earlier passage as the
actual beginning of the poem. This, from the internal evidence of the piece and its immediate

proximity to The Husband's Message, is probably what the Exeter Book scribe understood it to be - an integral part of what follows, perhaps even an introduction to it.

The fragment of 17 lines is not strictly riddlic in form since it does not possess the apparent contradictions that are meant to puzzle the hearer and which are considered essential features of riddles of this type. As F A Blackburn(8) pointed out, the object that speaks here is a letter and what follows in the manuscript is also the utterance of a letter represented as delivering its errand as a living messenger might do. M E Goldsmith(9) agrees that this must be so since The Husband's Message has something like a riddle opening but yet appears to be the continuation of a tale already begun.

Taken together then as a composite whole, the poem may be said to begin with a description of a reed growing by a lonely shore, that "knife edge and right hand, eorl's skill and point together joined" to fashion something intended to convey the runic message from the man (husband/lover) to his beloved (wife/betrothed). He appears to have been forced into exile "over the high seas" but has now found fortune, wealth and honour. In the urgent plea that he sends the woman through a trusted retainer, he bids her take ship once she has heard "on hillside's slope the melancholy cuckoo calling in the wood" and join him in his exile.

The poem closes with a kind of epilogue in which the woman is reminded of their former vows by the inscription in runes of what has been taken by N Kershaw(10) to represent the initials of the personal names of 'oath-helpers' but by others, notably R W V Elliott(11), to refer to the main themes of the poem presented in an expanded form by the rune-stave *(rúnakefli)* personified. Of the ancient vows of the husband and wife, he believes the messenger says "I hear heaven, earth and man declare together by oath that he would implement those pledges and those vows of love which you two often voiced in days gone by."

The Husband's Message, seen by Wrenn(12) to be mainly secular in tone like the other love-poems but with the usual Christian implications, and by Goldsmith(13) as a multiple allegory based on scriptural images, is not, in the final analysis, very markedly poetic, for it lacks the lyric intensity of feeling that characterizes **Wulf and Eadwacer** and The Wife's Lament.

The Wife's Lament, by coincidence, is exactly the same length as The Husband's Message. Some have therefore taken the two poems to relate to the same couple, although their content does not appear to confirm this view. Moreover, the poems are not placed together in the manuscript. That the speaker is a woman, is clear from the occurrence of feminine forms in the first two lines; whereas, in **Wulf and Eadwacer**, this is evident from the context. Both are love-poems, consisting of a single unintroduced speech.

The poem is a bitter indictment of a husband's betrayal of his spouse whom he has left to shift for herself on his departure for a distant land. She is compelled to dwell in a lonely cavern in a desolate grove by her husband's kindred who wish to keep them apart. In this place, she meditates on past happiness and present grief in material wretchedness. She finds the only friend she makes to be false - one who has probably also conspired to cause the rift between herself and her husband. She recalls the vows of lasting fidelity that she exchanged with her lord and is convinced that their love is "as though it never were." Vividly, but in general terms, she describes her present sojourn under an oak-tree in a cave-dwelling of ancient design, surrounded by high and inaccessible rocks, with dark, narrow valleys overgrown with briars. Here she weeps as she thinks of other lovers on earth who live in happiness and share a couch (37-41). And then she thinks of her husband who may possibly be miserable and grieving for her too. But finally her thought again returns to hopelessness, with the conclusion that "woe it is to him who out of longing must abide love" (52-3).

THE RUIN

24

25

THE RUIN

THE RUIN

Wrætlic is þes wealstan;   wyrde gebræcon,
burgstede burston,   brosnað enta geweorc.
Hrofas sind gehrorene,   hreorge torras,
hrungeat berofen,   hrim on lime,
scearde scurbeorge   scorene, gedrorene,
ældo undereotone.   Eorðgrap hafað
waldendwyhrtan,   forweorone, geleorene,
heard gripe hrusan,   oþ hund cnea
werþeoda gewitan.   Oft þæs wag gebad,
ræghar ond readfah,   rice æfter oþrum,
oftstonden under stormum;   steap geap gedreas.
Worað giet se[o] ....(r)um gehea[w]en,
felon u..........   ·...............e
grimme gegrunden   ....
.........(rð) scan   heo.................
............g orþonc,   ærsceaft........
..........g   lamrindum beag.
Mod mo[nade]   myne swiftne gebrægd;

The Ruin

Wondrous this wall-stone, wasted by fate;
city-halls crumbled; the work of giants decays.
Roofs are tumbled, towers ruined,
barred-gates broken, rime on lime lies,
storm-guards sheared, shivered, perished,
age-impaired. Earth's grasp imprisons
master-masons, mouldered, fled,
hard in grit's grip, till a hundred
generations pass. This wall stood long
goat-grey, red-stained, kingdoms rose and fell,
surviving storms; high curved arch crumbled.
Now moulders the ..... hewn
..... by files .....
grimly ground .....
..... shone
ancient work devised with skill
..... bent under crusts of mud.
A mind grew keen, swift purpose drew,

28

hwætred in hringas,   hygerof gebond
weallwalan wirum   wundrum togædre.
Beorht wæron burgræced,   burnsele monige,
heah horngestreon,   heresweg micel,
meodoheall monig   .ᛉ. dreama full,
oþþæt þæt onwende   wyrd seo swiþe.
Crungon walo wide,   cwoman woldagas,
swylt eall fornom   secgrofra wera;
wurdon hyra wigsteal   westenstaþolas,
brosnade burgsteall.   Betend crungon,
hergas to hrusan.   Forþon þas hofu dreorgiað
ond þæs teaforgeapa   tigelum sceadeð
hrostbeages [h]rof.   Hryre wong gecrong,
gebrocen to beorgum,   þær iu beorn monig,
glædmod ond goldbeorht,   gleoma gefrætwe[d],
wlonc ond wingal,   wighyrstum scan,
seah on sinc, on sylfor   on searogimmas,

resolute in rings, bound brave
its base with wondrous wires conjoint.
Bright were the city-halls, bath-houses many,
high wealth of gables, martial sound mighty,
many a mead-hall, full of men's revelry,
till fate the imperious altered that.
The slaughtered fell widely, pestilence followed;
death carried all those brave warriors away,
rendered their temples disconsolate places.
The city-state crumbled; rebuilders have fallen,
armies are dust. So these buildings grow desolate
and ochre tiles scatter
from woodwork of roof. The ruin crashed to earth,
reduced to rubble, where many a man once,
glad, gold-bright, in splendour geared,
proud, wine-flushed, in armour shone,
gazed on treasure, silver, rare gems,

on ead, on æht,   on eorcanstan,
on þas beorhtan burg   bradan rices.
Stanhofu stodan,   stream hate wearp
widan wylme;   weal eall befeng
beorhtan bosme;   þær þa baþu wæron,
hat on hreþre;   þæt wæs hyðelic.
Leton þonne geotan   (þ)...............
ofer harne stan   hate streamas
un(d).......... ....
oþþæt hringmere.   Hate (st)..........
....   þær þa baþu wæron.
....

riches, power, a precious jewel,
on this bright city in its broad realm.
Stone houses stood, the stream cast heat
in a wide surge; a wall enclosed all
in its bright bosom; there the baths were,
hot in the heart; that was convenient.
They let it pour then .....
over grey stone ..... hot streams .....
under ....
as far as that round pool. Hot .....
.... where the baths were.
....

32

THE WANDERER

34

THE WANDERER

THE WANDERER

Oft him anhaga   are gebideð,
Metudes miltse,   þeah þe he modcearig
geond lagulade   longe sceolde
hreran mid hondum   hrimcealde sæ,
wadan wræclastas: wyrd bið ful aræd!
  Swa cwæð eardstapa,   earfeþa gemyndig,
wraþra wælsleahta   winemæga hryre.
  Oft ic sceolde ana   uhtna gehwylce
mine ceare cwiþan -   nis nu cwicra nán
þe ic him modsefan   minne durre
sweotule asecgan.   Ic to soþe wat
þæt bið in eorle   indryhten þeaw
þæt he his ferðlocan   fæste binde,
healde his hordcofan,   hycge swa he wille.
  Ne mæg werig mod   wyrde wiðstondan,
ne se hreo hyge   helpe gefremman:
forðon domgeorne   dreorigne oft
in hyra breostcofan   bindað fæste,

The Wanderer

The solitary one solicits oft the grace,
the mercy of the Measurer, though sad at heart
across the watery way a weary while must he
stir with his hands the rime-cold sea,
tread exile tracks: full pitiless is fate!
    Thus quoth a wanderer, mindful of woes,
ferocious carnage, kinsmen massacred.
    Oft have I had alone at every dawn
my sorrows to lament - none living now is there
to whom my heart I dare
openly declare. I truly know
it is a noble custom in an *eorl*
that he bind fast his breast,
his broodings hold, think what he will.
    A weary mind withstands not fate,
nor does a rueful heart yield help:
hence those ambitious ofttimes sad
fast fetter in their breasts,

38

swa ic modsefan   minne sceolde
(oft earmcearig,   eðle bidæled,
freomægum feor)   feterum sælan,
siþþan geara iu   goldwine minne
hrusan heolstre biwrah,   ond ic hean þonan
wod wintercearig   ofer waþema gebind,
sohte seledreorig sinces bryttan,
hwær ic feor oþþe neah   findan meahte
þone þe in meoduhealle   minne myne wisse,
oþþe mec freondleasne   frefran wolde,
wenian mid wynnum.   Wat se þe cunnað
hu sliþen bið   sorg to geferan
þam þe him lyt hafað   leofra geholena:
warað hine wræclast,   nales wunden gold;
ferðloca freorig,   nalæs foldan blæd;
gemon he selesecgas   ond sincþege,
hu hine on geoguðe   his goldwine

as I should thoughts of mine
(oft careworn, of my native land deprived,
far from free kinsfolk) with shackles bind,
since long ago my lavish lord
in darkness earth enfolded, and I abject thence
fared winter-sad across the frozen waves,
sought sorrowful the hall of a gold-giver,
where I might find, or far or near,
him in mead-hall who would know my thought,
or comfort friendless me,
with kindness treat. He knows who trial makes
of grief how cruel a comrade it can be
for one who has few bosom friends:
the exile-track engrosses him, not twisted gold;
a frozen heart, not splendour of the earth;
he recalls retainers and receiving gifts,
how in his youth his lavish lord

wenede to wiste -   wyn eal gedreas!
Forþon wat se þe sceal   his winedryhtnes
leofes larcwidum   longe forþolian.
    Ðonne sorg ond slæp   somod ætgædre
earmne anhogan   oft gebindað,
þinceð him on mode   þæt he his mondryhten
clyppe ond cysse,   ond on cneo lecge
honda ond heafod,   swa he hwilum ær
in geardagum   giefstolas breac:
    ðonne onwæcneð eft   wineleas guma,
gesihð him biforan   fealwe wægas,
baþian brimfuglas,   brædan feþra,
hreosan hrim ond snaw   hagle gemenged.
þonne beoð þy hefigran   heortan benne,
sare æfter swæsne -   sorg bið geniwad -
þonne maga gemynd   mod geondhweorfeð,
greteð gliwstafum,   georne geondsceawað.
Secga geseldan   swimmað eft onweg,
fleotendra ferð   no þær fela bringeð
cuðra cwidegiedda -   cearo bið geniwad -

was wont to feasting him - that joy has perished quite!
This he knows who must his friendly lord's
beloved precepts long forgo.
  When together grief and sleep
the wretched reculse often bind,
in thought to him it seems his liege lord he
is clasping, kissing, laying upon his knee
his hands and head, as whilom he
in days of yore the gift-throne's boons enjoyed:
  then wakes the friendless man again,
sees before him fallow waves,
bathing sea-birds, preening wings,
frost and snow hail-mingled fall.
Heavier are the heart's wounds then,
for his beloved sore - sorrow is renewed -
when the memory of kinsmen crosses his mind
he greets them gleefully, eagerly watches
his warrior comrades; they drift away again.
The spirit of seafarers brings there not many
familiar songs - care is renewed -

þam þe sendan sceal   swiþe geneahhe
ofer waþema gebind   werigne sefan.
    Forþon ic geþencan ne mæg   geond þas woruld
forhwan modsefa   min ne gesweorce,
þonne ic eorla lif   eal geondþence,
hu hi færlice   flet ofgeafon,
modge maguþegnas,   swa þes middangeard
ealra dogra gehwam   dreoseð ond fealleþ.
Forþon ne mæg wearþan wis   wer, ær he age
wintra dæl in woruldrice.   Wita sceal geþyldig:
ne sceal no to hatheort,   ne to hrædwyrde,
ne to wac wiga,   ne to wanhydig,
ne to forht, ne to fægen,   ne to feohgifre,
ne næfre gielpes to georn   ær he geare cunne:
beorn sceal gebidan,   þonne he beot spriceð,
oþþæt, collenferð,   cunne gearwe
hwider hreþra gehygd   hweorfan wille.

to him who oft enough must send
over the frozen waves his weary heart.
  And so I cannot think why in this world
my spirit grows not sad,
when I consider close the life of *eorls*,
how suddenly they yielded up the hall,
high-spirited young thanes; just so, this middle-earth
fails each and every day and falls.
Assuredly, a man may not turn wise, ere he possess
his share of winters in the world. A wise man must be calm:
he must neither be too passionate, nor too rash of speech,
nor too weak a warrior, nor too precipitate,
nor too timid, nor too eager, nor too greedy for gain,
never to boast too keen, ere he know well:
a man must wait, when vow he makes,
until, for action fit, he truly knows
whither his heart's aims will incline.

Ongietan sceal gleaw hæle   hu gæstlic bið,
þonne ealre þisse worulde wela   weste stondeð,
swa nu missenlice   geond þisne middangeard,
winde biwaune,   weallas stondaþ
hrime bihrorene,   hryðge þa ederas.
Woniað þa winsalo,   waldend licgað
dreame bidrorene,   duguþ eal gecrong
wlonc bi wealle.   Sume wig fornom,
ferede in forðwege: sumne fugel oþbær
ofer heanne holm;   sumne se hara wulf
deaðe gedælde;   sumne dreorighleor
in eorðscræfe   eorl gehydde.
Yþde swa þisne eardgeard   ælda Scyppend
oþþæt, burgwara   breahtma lease,
eald enta geweorc   idlu stodon.

Se þonne þisne wealsteal   wise geþohte,
ond þis deorce lif · deope geondþenceð,
frod in ferðe,   feor oft gemon
wælsleahta worn,   ond þas word acwið:
Hwær cwom mearg? Hwær cwom mago?   Hwær cwom
          maþþumgyfa?

A prudent hero must perceive how hideous it will be,
when all this world of wealth stands waste,
as now, in varied places through this middle-earth,
blown on by winds, stand walls
rime-girt, the courts snow-swept.
The wine halls crumble, lords lie low
deprived of mirth, the doughty troop all dead
brave by the wall. War wasted one,
fetched him away: one the bird bore
across the deep sea; one the hoar wolf
rent to death; one sad of mien,
in cave of earth, a warrior hid.
Thus did the Creator of men lay waste this world
until, bereft of their folk's revelry,
the ancient work of giants idle stood.
  Then he who wisely ponders this foundation-wall,
and deeply thinks on every aspect of this darksome life,
sage in spirit, oft from far recalls
the many battles, and declares these words:
Where is the steed gone? Where is the rider? where is
        the giver of gifts?

Hwær cwom symbla gesetu?   Hwær sindon seledreamas?
Eala beorht bune!   Eala byrnwiga!
Eala þeodnes þrym!   Hu seo þrag gewat,
genap under nihthelm,   swa heo no wære!
      Stondeð nu on laste   leofre duguþe
weal wundrum heah   wyrmlicum fah -
eorlas fornoman   asca þryþe,
wæpen wælgifru,   wyrd seo mære -
ond þas stanhleoþu   stormas cnyssað;
hrið hreosende   hrusan bindeð;
wintres woma   (þonne won cymeð,
nipeð, nihtscua)   norþan onsendeð
hreo hæglfare   hæleþum on andan.
      Eall is earfoðlic   eorþan rice:
onwendeð wyrda gesceaft   weoruld under heofonum.
Her bið feoh læne,   her bið freond læne,

Where are the banqueting seats? Where are the joys of hall?
Alas the bright goblet! Alas the mailed warrior!
Alas the lord's majesty! How that time's passed away,
grown dark neath shades of night, as though it never were!
    There stands as token now to that beloved troop
a wondrous high wall, decked with serpent shapes -
a host of spears snatched away the *eorls*,
weapons greedy for carnage, a glorious fate -
and storms strike these stony slopes;
the falling snow-storm fetters the earth;
winter's tumult (when the darkness comes,
casts gloom, the shades of night) sends from the north
fierce driving hail in malice towards men.
    All the realm of earth is wearisome:
the decree of fate changes the world beneath the sky.
Here wealth is brief, here friend short-lived,

48

her bið mon læne,   her bið mæg læne;
eal þis eorþan gesteal   idel weorþeð.
    Swa cwæð snottor on mode,   gesæt him sundor æt rune.
Til biþ se þe his treowe gehealdeþ.   Ne sceal næfre his
        torn to rycene
beorn of his breostum acyþan,   nemþe he ær þa bote
        cunne,
eorl, mid elne gefremman.   Wel bið þam þe him are seceð,
frofre to Fæder on heofonum,   þær us eal seo fæstnung
        stondeð.

49

here man is frail, here kinsman is infirm;
all this earth's constitution comes to naught.
*Thus quoth a wise man in his heart, in meditation as he sat
apart.*
Blest is he who keeps his troth. Never must too hastily the wrath
a warrior from the heart express, unless the *eorl* know first the
cure,
with courage to effect. It will be well for him who mercy seeks,
comfort from the Father in the firmament, where for us all the
immutable abides.

50

THE SEAFARER

52

THE SEAFARER

THE SEAFARER

Mæg ic be me sylfum soðgied wrecan,
siþas secgan, hu ic geswincdagum
earfoðhwile oft þrowade,
bitre breostceare gebiden hæbbe,
gecunnad in ceole cearselda fela,
atol yþa gewealc, þær mec oft bigeat
nearo nihtwaco æt nacan stefnan,
þonne he be clifum cnossað. Calde geþrungen
wæron mine fet, forste gebunden
caldum clommum, þær ceare seofedun
hat ymb heortan; hungor innan slat
merewerges mod. þæt se mon ne wat
þe him on foldan fægrost limpeð,
hu ic earmcearig iscealdne sæ
winter wunade wræccan lastum,
winemægum bidroren,
bihongen hrimgicelum; hægl scurum fleag.
þær ic ne gehyrde butan hlimman sæ,

The Seafarer

Of myself, a true tale I can tell,
recount my trials, how in times of toil
I often suffered sore,
how I bitter-breast cares bore,
many sites of sorrow tried in ships,
terrible the tossing waves, where I kept oft
the narrow night-watch at the vessel's prow,
when by the cliff it bolts. Constricted with the cold
my feet were, bound with frost's
chill fetters, where lamented care
hot round my heart, where hunger inly rent
the ocean-weary spirit. He, whose lot
is cast most happily on land, knows not
how, careworn, I upon that ice-cold sea
endured long the exile tracks,
destitute of kinsmen,
icicle engirt; in showers flew hail.
There I heard naught except the roaring sea,

56

iscaldne wæg.   Hwilum ylfete song
dyde ic me to gomene,   ganetes hleoþor
ond huilpan sweg   fore hleahtor wera,
mæw singende   fore medodrince.
Stormas þær stanclifu beotan,   þær him stearn oncwæð
isigfeþera;   ful oft þæt earn bigeal,
urigfeþra;   nænig hleomæga
feasceaftig ferð   frefran meahte.

   For þon him gelyfeð lyt,   se þe ah lifes wyn
gebiden in burgum,   bealosiþa hwon,
wlonc ond wingal,   hu ic werig oft
in brimlade   bidan sceolde.
Nap nihtscua,   norþan sniwde,
hrim hrusan bond,   hægl feol on eorþan,
corna caldast.   For þon cnyssað nu
heortan geþohtas   þæt hean streamas,

the ice-cold wave. Whilom the wild swan's song
I had for cheer, the gannet's cry
and curlew's music stead of merriment of men,
the seagull's singing stead of drinking mead.
Storms beat the stone cliffs there, and there the tern
        re-echoed them
icy-winged; oft the eagle screamed around,
dewy-winged; protecting kinsmen none
the wretched heart might there console.
    Forsooth he scarce believes, who has life's joys
in cities relished, from misfortune free,
inspirited and flushed with wine, how ofttimes weary I
have had to bide the ocean-path.
The shades of night grow dark, and northerly it snowed,
frost fettered earth, hail fell upon the ground,
coldest of grains. So now oppress
my heart the thoughts that I the towering seas,

sealtyþa gelac   sylf cunnige -
monað modes lust   mæla gehwylce
ferð to feran,   þæt ic feor heonan
elþeodigra   eard gesece -
for þon nis þæs modwlonc   mon ofer eorþan,
ne his gifena þæs god,   ne in geoguþe to þæs hwæt,
ne in his dædum to þæs deor,   ne him his dryhten to þæs hold,
þæt he a his sæfore   sorge næbbe,
to hwon hine Dryhten   gedon wille.
Ne biþ him to hearpan hyge   ne to hringþege -
ne to wife wyn   ne to worulde hyht -
ne ymbe owiht elles   nefne ymb yða gewealc;
ac a hafað longunge   se þe on lagu fundað.
Bearwas blostmum nimað,   byrig fægriað,
wongas wlitigað,   woruld onetteð;
ealle þa gemoniað   modes fusne
sefan to siþe   þam þe swa þenceð
on flodwegas   feor gewitan.
Swylce geac monað   geomran reorde;
singeð sumeres weard,   sorge beodeð

the salt waves' tumult must myself explore -
the heart's desire exhorts each time
the thought to fare, that I far hence
should seek an alien land -
because there is no man so proud of heart on earth,
nor of his gifts so generous, nor in his youth so bold,
nor in his deeds so brave, nor with a lord so kind to him
that never has he fear for his sea-voyaging,
concerning what the Lord apportions him.
His thought is not for harp nor taking of rings -
nor happiness in wife nor joy in worldly things -
nor for aught else, save the surging waves;
but ever does he yearn who seeks the sea.
The groves bear blossoms, the towns turn lovely,
the fields grow fair, the world revives;
all these urge to fare afar
the eager heart and mind of him who thinks
upon the sea-ways to depart.
The cuckoo likewise prompts with melancholy voice;
the harbinger of summer sings, and sorrow bodes

60

bitter in breosthord.　Þæt se beorn ne wat,
sefteadig secg,　hwæt þa sume dreogað
þe þa wræclastas　widost lecgað.
　　For þon nu min hyge hweorfeð　ofer hreþerlocan,
min modsefa　mid mereflode,
ofer hwæles eþel　hweorfeð wide,
eorþan sceatas,　cymeð eft to me
gifre ond grædig;　gielleð anfloga,
hweteð on hwælweg　hreþer unwearnum
ofer holma gelagu,　for þon me hatran sind
Dryhtnes dreamas　þonne þis deade lif
læne on londe.
　　　　　　　　Ic gelyfe no
þæt him eorðwelan　ece stondað.
Simle þreora sum　þinga gehwylce
ær his tiddege　to tweon weorþeð:
adl oþþe yldo　oþþe ecghete

a bitter breast-hoard. That the man knows not,
the man with comfort blest, what some of those endure
who tread the farthest exile-tracks.
  So now my heart beyond its confines roves,
my spirit with the flood
wide over whale's haunt fares,
and earth's expanse, comes back to me
avid and insatiate; the lone flier screams,
irresistibly the heart whets to the whale-way
over the stretch of seas. For more fervid to me
are the Lord's joys than this dead life
ephemeral on land.
              I think not true
that earthly weal endures eternally.
Ever each of these three things
in doubt stands till his destined hour:
disease, or age, or violence of war

62

fægum fromweardum   feorh oðþringeð.
For þon biþ eorla gehwam   æftercweþendra
lof lifgendra   lastworda betst,
þæt he gewyrce,   ær he on weg scyle,
fremum on foldan   wið feonda niþ,
deorum dædum   deofle togeanes,
þæt hine ælda bearn   æfter hergen,
ond his lof siþþan   lifge mid englum
awa to ealdre,   ecan lifes blæd,
dream mid dugeþum.

                            Dagas sind gewitene,
ealle onmedlan   eorþan rices;
nearon nu cyningas   ne caseras
ne goldgiefan   swylce iu wæron,
þonne hi mæst mid him   mærþa gefremedon
ond on dryhtlicestum   dome lifdon.
Gedroren is þeos duguð eal,   dreamas sind gewitene;
wuniað þa wacran   ond þas woruld healdaþ.

will wrest life from the fated man.
And so for every warrior posterity's
continued praise is the best epitaph,
that he may earn, ere he must go,
by good on earth against the enmity of friends,
with noble deeds the devil to defeat,
so that the sons of men will praise him afterwards,
and then his glory with the angels live
for evermore, in splendour of eternal life,
bliss among that multitude.
                                    Those days are fled,
all the grandeur of earth's realm;
neither kings nor Caesars now
nor gold-givers are such as were of yore,
when they amongst themselves the greatest deeds of glory wrought
and lived in lordliest renown.
All fallen is this noble troop, the joys are fled;
the decadent survive and hold this world,

brucað þurh bisgo. Blæd is gehnæged,
eorþan indryhto   ealdað ond searað,
swa nu monna gehwylc   geond middangeard.
Yldo him on fareð,   onsyn blacað,
gomelfeax gnornað,   wat his iuwine,
æþelinga bearn   eorþan forgiefene.
Ne mæg him þonne se flæschoma,   þonne him þæt feorg losað,
ne swete forswelgan   ne sar gefelan
ne hond onhreran   ne mid hyge þencan.
Þeah þe græf wille   golde stregan
broþor his geborenum,   byrgan be deadum
maþmum mislicum,   þæt hine mid nille,
ne mæg þære sawle   þe bið synna ful
gold to geoce   for Godes egsan,
þonne he hit ær hydeð   þenden he her leofað.
    Micel bið se Meotudes egsa,   for þon hi seo molde oncyrreð;
se gestaþelade   stiþe grundas,
eorþan sceatas   ond uprodor.
Dol bið se þe him his Dryhten ne ondrædeþ: cymeð him se deað
    unþinged.

possess it in affliction. Glory is abased,
earth's nobleness grows old and stales,
as every man now does throughout the middle-earth.
Old age comes on him, his face grows pale,
grey-haired he grieves, he knows his friends of yore,
the sons of princes have been given up to earth.
When life fails him, then may his corpse
nor sweetness taste nor pain sustain
nor move a hand nor think with mind.
Though brother he will strew with gold the grave
of brother born, and with the dead inter
assorted treasures, that they go with him,
yet may the soul that is replete with sin
be aided not by gold before God's wrath,
although he hoards it here while he yet lives.
   Great is God's might, before which earth will turn aside;
its firm foundations He decreed,
the earth's expanse and the sky above.
Foolish is he who does not fear his Lord: death to him comes
         unforeseen.

Eadig bið se þe eaþmod leofaþ;   cymeð him seo ar of heofonum.
Meotod him þæt mod gestaþelað,   for þon he in his meahte gelyfeð.
Stieran mon sceal strongum mode,   ond þæt on staþelum healdan,
ond gewis werum,   wisum clæne.
Scyle monna gehwylc   mid gemete healdan
wiþ leofne ond wið laþne   ***** bealo.
Þeah he ne wille   fyres fulne
oþþe on bæle   forbærnedne
his geworhtne wine,   Wyrd biþ swiþre,
Meotud meahtigra,   þonne ænges monnes gehygd.
Uton we hycgan   hwær we ham agen,
ond þonne geþencan   hu we þider cumen;
ond we þonne eac tilien   þæt we to moten
in þa ecan   eadignesse
þær is lif gelong   in lufan Dryhtnes,
hyht in heofonum.   þæs sy þam Halgan þonc
þæt he usic geweorþade,   wuldres Ealdor
ece Dryhten,   in ealle tid.
                                    Amen.

Blest is he who humbly lives; to him from heaven mercy comes;
God makes that mood steadfast in him for in His might he trusts.
With strong mind must a man himself control, and firmly hold to
        that,
be constant towards men, and pure in every wise.
Let every man in moderation hold
with friend and with pernicious foe.
Though he desire not with fire to be filled
or in the conflagration to be quite consumed
his friend acquired, Fate is stronger far,
God mightier, than any man's imagining.
Let us consider where we have our home,
and then reflect how we may thither get;
and when moreover we may labour that we be allowed
into eternal blessedness
where is the source of life in love of God,
hope in the heavens. Through all time
be thanks to holy God, the Prince of Glory,
Lord eternal, that He exalted us.
              Amen.

68

DEOR

DEOR

DEOR

Welund him be wurman   wræces cunnade.
Anhydig eorl,   earfoþa dreag,
hæfde him to gesiþþe   sorge ond longaþ,
wintercealde wræce;   wean oft onfond
siþþan hine Niðhad on   nede legde,
swoncre seonobende,   on syllan monn.
    þæs ofereode;   þisses swa mæg.

Beodohilde ne wæs   hyre broþra deaþ
on sefan swa sár   swa hyre sylfre þing,
þæt heo gearolice   ongieten hæfde
þæt heo eacen wæs;   æfre ne meahte
þriste geþencan   hu ymb þæt sceolde.
    þæs ofereode;   þisses swa mæg.

Deor

Welund, entramelled, understood wrack.
He, stubborn hero, suffered privation,
had, as companions, sorrow and longing,
a wintry-cold exile; he oft found woes
once *Nithhad* laid need on him,
lithe sinew-bonds on the better man.
    That passed away; so may this.

Beadohild wasn't for her brother's deaths
so sore in spirit as for her own state,
in that too plainly she had perceived
that she was pregnant; nor ever could she
consider boldly what should become of that.
    That passed away; so may this.

We þæt Hæðhilde   mone gefrugnon
wurdon grundlease   Geates frige,
þæt hi seo sorglufu   slæp ealle binom.
   þæs ofereode;   þisses swa mæg.

Ðeodric ahte   þritig wintra
Mæringa burg;   þæt wæs monegum cuþ.
   þæs ofereode;   þisses swa mæg.

We geascodan   Eormanrices
wylfenne geþoht;   ahte wide folc
Gotena rices.   þæt wæs grim cyning.
Sæt secg monig   sorgum gebunden,
wean on wenan,   wyscte geneahhe
þæt þæs cynerices   ofercumen wære.
   þæs ofereode;   þisses swa mæg.

Of *Maethhild* many of us have heard tell
the *Geat's* affection for her became boundless,
that their hapless love wholly reft them of sleep.
    That passed away; so may this.

For thirty years *Theodric* held
the Maerings' stronghold; to many was that known.
    That passed away; so may this.

We have heard of *Eormanric's*
wolfish design; widely he held folk
of the kingdom of Goths. That was a grim king.
Many a man would sit shackled with sorrows,
in prospect of woe, and earnestly wish
that his rule were restricted.
    That passed away; so may this.

76

Siteð sorgcearig,   sælum bidæled,
on sefan sweorceð;   sylfum þinceð
þæt sy endeleas   earfoða dæl.
Mæg þonne geþencan   þæt geond þas woruld
witig Dryhten   wendeþ geneahhe,
eorle monegum   are gesceawað,
wislicne blæd,   sumum weana dæl.
þæt ic bi me sylfum   secgan wille,
þæt ic hwile wæs   Heodeninga scop,
dryhtne dyre.   Me wæs Deor noma.
Ahte ic fela wintra   folgað tilne,
holdne hlaford,   oþþæt Heorrenda nú,
leoðcræftig monn,   londrhyt geþah
þæt me eorla hleo   ær gesealde.

      þæs ofereode: þisses swa mæg.

The sorrowful one sits deprived of delight,
in spirit grows dark; to him it seems
that his share of sufferings is without end.
He may then wonder that all through this world
the wise Lord wends constant,
to many a man grants grace,
certain success, countless sorrows to some.
Of myself I will say that
the *scop* of the *Heodeningas* once I was,
dear to my prince. *Deor* was my name.
For many a winter I had meet office,
a loyal lord, until *Heorrenda* now,
a man skilled in song, received the land-rights
that the refuge of warriors erst rendered me.

    That passed away; so may this.

78

WULF AND EADWACER

WULF AND EADWACER

WULF AND EADWACER

Leodum is minum   swylce him mon lac gife;
willað hy hine aþecgan,   gif he on þreat cymeð?
   Ungelic is us.
Wulf is on iege,   ic on oþerre.
Fæst is þæt eglond,   fenne biworpen.
Sindon wælreowe   weras þær on ige.
Willað hy hine aþecgan,   gif he on þreat cymeð?
   Ungelic is us.
Wulfes ic mines widlastum   wenum dogode;
þonne hit wæs renig weder   ond ic reotugu sæt,
þonne mec se beaducafa   bogum bilegde,
wæs me wyn to þon,   wæs me hwæþre eac lað.
Wulf, min Wulf,   wena me þine
seoce gedydon,   þine seldcymas,
murnende mod,   nales meteliste.
Gehyrest þu, Eadwacer?   Uncerne earne hwelp
bireð wulf to wuda.
Þæt mon eaþe tosliteð   þætte næfre gesomnad wæs,
uncer giedd geador.

Wulf and Eadwacer

To my folk it is as though one might give them a gift;
will they receive him, if he comes as a threat?
    Our lots are different.
Wulf is on one isle, I on another.
That isle is secure, surrounded by fens.
Bloodthirsty men are there on that isle.
Will they receive him, if he comes as a threat?
    Our lots are different.
My *Wulf's* far-wanderings I suffered, hopeful;
when the weather was rainy and I weeping sat;
when the brave warrior wound his arms round me;
there was delight in it, yet also disgust.
Wulf, my *Wulf*, my thwarted hopes of seeing thee
have made me sick, the rareness of thy visits,
my woeful mood, not want of food.
Hearest thou, *Eadwacer?* Our wretched whelp
Wulf shall bear off to the wood.
That is easily severed that never was joined:
the riddle of us two together.

85

THE HUSBAND'S MESSAGE

THE HUSBAND'S MESSAGE

THE HUSBAND'S MESSAGE

Ic wæs be sonde,   sæwealle neah,
æt merefaroþe,   minum gewunade
frumstaþole fæst;   fea ænig wæs
monna cynnes,   þæt minne þær
on anæde   eard beheolde,
ac mec uhtna gehwam   yð sio brune
lagufæðme beleolc.   Lyt ic wende
þæt ic ær oþþe sið   æfre sceolde
ofer meodubence   muðleas sprecan,
wordum wrixlan.   þæt is wundres dæl,
on sefan searolic   þam þe swylc ne conn,
hu mec seaxes ord   ond seo swiþre hond,
eorles ingeþonc   ond ord somod,
þingum geþydan,   þæt ic wiþ þe sceolde
for unc anum twam   ærendspræce
abeodan bealdlice,   swa hit beorna ma
uncre wordcwidas   widdor ne mænden.

The Husband's Message

On the shore I was, the sea-wall nigh,
in the sea-waves; I abode
firm-rooted in my first home. Few
human beings were there who marked
my solitary dwelling-place;
but every dawn the dark wave locked
me in its watery embrace. I little thought
that I should ever, at any time,
over the head, speak, mouthless,
swap speech. A wonder great it is,
strange to the minds of them that do not know,
how knife edge and right hand,
eorl's skill and point together,
joined, that I to thee should,
before us two alone, my message
boldly tell, that other men may not
our discourse bruit abroad.

Nu ic onsundran þe   secgan wille
......(n) treocyn.   Ic tudre aweox;
in mec æld[a].....   ..... sceal
ellor londes setta(n)   ....lc,
sealte streamas   ....sse.
Ful oft ic on bates [bosme]   ...... gesohte,
þær mec mondryhten   min ....
ofer heah h[a]fu;   eom nu her cumen
on ceolþele,   ond nu cunnan scealt
hu þu ymb modluf[a]n   mines frean
on hyge hycge.   Ic gehatan dear
þæt þu þær tirfæste   treowe findest.
    Hwæt, þec þonne biddan het,   se þisne beam agrof,
þæt þu sinchroden   sylf gemunde
on gewitlocan   wordbeotunga
þe git on ærdagum   oft gespræcon,
þenden git moston   on meoduburgum
eard weardigan,   an lond bugan,

91

Now I will tell thee privately
..... a kind of tree. I waxed in infancy;
on me ..... men ..... must
in alien lands set .....
salt streams ..... Oft by boat I
..... sought
where my lord ..... me
over the high seas. I have come now
on shipboard here; and, now thou shalt know
how thou mayest think of my lord's love
in thy mind. I dare declare
that thou wilt find a firm faith there.
    Lo, then, he that graved this wood bade me pray thee
that thou, bejewelled, thyself recall
to mind these spoken vows
that ye two uttered oft in former days,
while ye together yet in mead-halls might
your habitation hold, in one land dwell,

freondscype fremman.   Hine fæhþo adraf
of sigeþeode.   Heht nu sylfa þe
lustum læra[n]   þæt þu lagu drefde,
siþþan þu gehyrde   on hliþes oran
galan geomorne   geac on bearwe.
Ne læt þu þec siþþan   siþes getwæfan,
lade gelettan,   lifgendne monn.
     Ongin mere secan,   mæwes eþel.
Onsite sænacan,   þæt þu suð heonan
ofer merelade   monnan findest,
þær se þeoden is   þin on wenum.
Ne mæg him [on] worulde   willa [gelimpan]
mara on gemyndum,   þæsþe he me sægde,
þonne inc geunne   alwaldend God,
[þæt git] ætsomne   siþþan motan
secgum ond gesiþum   s[inc brytnian],
nægledebeagas.   He genoh hafað
fædan gold[es], ...

your friendship forward. Him a fued drove away
from his victorious people. Now he himself has bidden me
joyfully to urge thee stir the sea,
once thou hast heard on hiilside's slope
the melancholy cuckoo calling in the wood.
Thereafter, do not thou be stayed from journeying,
hindered in thy going, by any living man.
   Seek the deep, the sea-mew's home.
Take ship so that thou southward hence,
beyond the mere-track, findest thy man,
where lives thy lord in hopes of thee.
No greater wish in this world comes
to his mind more, he told me so,
than that all-wielding God should grant
that later ye together may
dispense, to warriors and to comrades, wealth,
studded rings. He hath enough
of burnished gold ....

[geon]d elþeode   eþel healde,
fægre fold[an]   ....
[hold]ra hæleþa,   þeahþe her min win(e)
....
nyde gebæded,   nacan ut aþrong,
ond on yþa gel(a)g[u   ana] sceolde
faran on flotweg,   forðsiþes georn,
mengan merestreamas.   Nu se mon hafað
wean oferwunnen;   nis him wilna gad,
ne meara, ne maðma,   ne meododreama
ænges ofer eorþan   eorlgestreona,
þeodnes dohtor,   gif he þin beneah.
Ofer eald gebeot   incer twega,
gehyre ic ætsomne   . ᛄ . ᚱ . geador
. ᚹ . ᛈ . ond . ᚻ .   aþe benemnan
þæt he þa wære   ond þa winetreowe,
be him lifgendum   læstan wolde,
þe git on ærdagum   oft gespræconn.

though he among an alien race his dwelling holds,
a lovely land ....
trusty heroes, even here my lord
....
by need compelled, his boat launched out
and on the sea-swell had to journey lone,
fare on the flood, eager to escape,
stir the sea-streams. Now hath the man
vanquished woes; he lacks not his desires,
nor steeds nor wealth, nor mead-delights,
none of the treasures of *eorls* on earth,
O prince's daughter, if he possess thee
as vouchsafed by the ancient vow of both of you.
I hear both S and R conjoined
with EA, W and M on oath aver
that he, the pledge and cordial covenant,
his living self would keep,
that ye two uttered oft in former days.

H2

96

THE WIFE'S LAMENT

98

99

THE WIFE'S LAMENT

THE WIFE'S LAMENT

Ic þis giedd wrece   bi me ful geomorre,
minre sylfre sið.   Ic þæt secgan mæg
hwæt ic yrmþa gebad,   siþþan ic up [a]weox,
niwes oþþe ealdes,   no ma þonne nu.
A ic wite wonn   minra wræcsiþa.
     Ærest min hlaford gewat   heonan of leodum
ofer yþa gelac.   Hæfde ic uhtceare
hwær min leodfruma   londes wære.
Ða ic me feran gewat   folgað secan,
wineleas wræcca,   for minre weaþearfe,
ongunnon þæt þæs monnes   magas hycgan
þurh dyrne geþoht,   þæt hy todælden unc,
þæt wit gewidost   in woruldrice
lifdon laðlicost;   ond mec longade.
     Het mec hlaford min   her eard niman;
ahte ic leofra lyt   on þissum londstede,
holdra freonda;   forþon is min hyge geomor.

The Wife's Lament

Full sadly this song I sing of myself,
of my own fate. I can affirm
what trials I bore, since I grew up,
or new or old, were never more than now.
Ever I suffer the pain of my exile.

    First my lord from his folk hence
over the wild waves went. Dawn-cares I had
as to where my lord in the land might be.
When I set out a retinue to seek,
friendless exile, for my woeful plight,
that man's relatives began to plot,
through secret schemes, to sunder us,
so that most widely in this world apart
we should dwell wretched; I was ill at ease.

    My lord bade me my dwelling here to hold;
loved and loyal friends in this land I
owned few; for this my soul is sad.

Ða ic me ful gemæcne   monnan funde,
heardsæligne,   hygegeomorne,
mod miþendne,   morþor hycgend[n]e,
bliþe gebæro.   Ful oft wit beotedan
þæt unc ne gedælde   nemne deað ana,
owiht elles;   eft is þæt onhworfen.
Is nu [fornumen]   swa hit no wære,
freondscipe uncer.   S[c]eal ic feor ge neah
mines felaleofan   fæhðu dreogan.
    Heht mec mon wunian   on wuda bearwe,
under actreo   in þam eorðscræfe.
Eald is þes eorðsele;   eal is eom oflongad;
sindon dena dimme,   duna uphea,
bitre burgtunas   brerum beweaxne,
wic wynna leas.   Ful oft mec her wraþe begat
fromsiþ frean.   Frynd sind on eorþan,
leofe lifgende,   leger weardiað,
þonne ic on uhtan   ana gonge
under actreo   geond þas eorðscrafu.

When I had found a well-matched man,
ill-starred, melancholy-minded,
his dissembling heart was plotting homicide
with pleasant mien. Full oft we pledged,
save death alone, naught should divide
us else; that is altered now.
Now is destroyed, as though it never were,
our friendship. Far or near I must
endure the fued of my much-loved one.
    They bade me dwell in a wooded grove,
under an oak-tree, in this earth-cave.
Old this earth-hall; I all longing filled;
dales are dim, hills high,
cities choked with bitter briars,
dwellings joyless. Here I am full oft beset
by my lord's going. Friends there are on earth,
lovers living, who lie abed,
when I, at daybreak, walk alone,
under oak-trees, through these earth-caves.

þær ic sittan mot   sumorlangne dæg,
þær ic wepan mæg   mine wræcsiþas,
earfoþa fela;   forþon ic æfre ne mæg
þære modceare   minre gerestan,
ne ealles þæs longaþes   þe mec on þissum life begeat.
    A scyle geong mon   wesan geomormod,
heard heortan geþoht;   swylce habban sceal
bliþe gebæro,   eac þon breostceare,
sinsorgna gedreag,   sy æt him sylfum gelong
eal his worulde wyn.   Sy ful wide fah
feorres folclondes,   þæt min freond siteð
under stanhliþe   storme behrimed,
wine werigmod,   wætre beflowen
on dreorsele.   Dreogeð se min wine
micle modceare;   he gemon to oft
wynlicran wic.   Wa bið þam þe sceal
of langoþe   leofes abidan.

There must I sit the summer's day long,
where my exile-ways I mourn,
my many woes, for I never can
my careworn self compose.
nor all the longing in me that this life begat.
 Ever shall that youth be sad of mood,
pained his brooding heart; he shall sustain,
besides a cheerful mien, breast-cares as well,
endure incessant griefs; let him depend upon himself
for all his worldly joy. Let him be cast adrift,
afar in a distant land, that he, my friend, may sit
neath stony slopes, by storms berimed,
my evil-minded comrade, water drenched
in drear dwelling. My comrade will endure
great grief; too often he will think
upon a happier home. Woe is it to him
who out of longing must abide love.

106

NOTES

Introduction

1 C L Wrenn, *A Study of Old English Literature* (London, 1967), p. 140.
2 S B Greenfield and D G Calder, *A New Critical History of Old English Literature* (New York, 1968), p. 281.
3 C L Wrenn, loc. cit.
4 T A Shippey, *Old English Verse* (London, 1970), p. 53.
5 C L Wrenn, op. cit., p. 81.
6 T A Shippey, op. cit., p. 75.
7 Kemp Malone, 'Two English *Frauenlieder*,' in *Studies in Old English Literature in Honor of Arthur Brodeur* (University of Oregon, 1963, pp. 106-11).
8 F A Blackburn, '*The Husband's Message* and the Accompanying Riddles of the Exeter Book,' *JEGP* (1901), iii, 1-13.
9 M E Goldsmith, 'The Enigma of *The Husband's Message*,' in *Anglo-Saxon Poetry: Essays in Appreciation. For John C McGalliard* (University of Notre Dame, 1975), pp. 242-63.
10 N Kershaw, *Anglo-Saxon and Norse Poems* (Cambridge, 1922), p. 42, fn.2.
11 R W V Elliott, 'The Runes in *The Husband's Message*,' *JEGP* (1955), liv, 1-8.
12 C L Wrenn, op. cit., p. 152.
13 M E Goldsmith, loc. cit.

NOTES (continued)

Deor

1 Welund, the mythical smith of Germanic legend, Volundr in the *Vǫlundarkviđa*, Daedalus or Vulcan in classical mythology.

5 Niđhad, or Niđuđr, King of the Niarar, in the *Vǫlundarkviđa*.

8 Beadohild, or Bođvildr, in the *Vǫlundarkivđa*, the daughter of Niđhad. Welund slew her two brothers and ravished her to avenge himself on Niđhad. Widia, her son by Welund, is mentioned in the poem *Waldere* (I, 6).

14 Maeđhild is identified by Kemp Malone (in his edition of *Deor*, p. 8) with Magnhild, the herione of a Scandinavian ballad.

15 Geat, the hero of the ballad afore-mentioned, is there known as Gaute or Gauti.

18 Đeodric, king of the Visigoths, or Maeringas (19).

21 Eormanric, or Ermanaricus, King of the Ostrogoths, flourished in the third quarter of the fourth century A.D.

36 Heodeningas, a royal family which claimed descent from Heoden whose tribe was the Glomman, according to the poem *Widsith* (21).

37 Deor, not mentioned elsewhere, probably an invention of the author's, like the minstrel of *Widsith*.

38 Heorrenda, according to Kemp Malone (op. cit., p40) seems to be the Hjarrandi of Icelandic tradition, whose Danish equivalent, Hjarne, is the minstrel king of Saxo's *Gesta Danorum*.

Also published by Llanerch:

ANGLO-SAXON RIDDLES
translated by
Louis Rodrigues.

AN ANGLO-SAXON GENESIS
translated by
Lawrence Mason
with illustrations from
the Junius manuscript.

BEOWULF
translated by
John Porter
with illustrations by
Nicholas Parry.

NORTHUMBRIAN CROSSES
OF THE PRE-NORMAN AGE
by W. G. Collingwood.

A HISTORY OF THE KINGS
by Florence of Worcester.

From booksellers. For a complete list,
write to: Llanerch Publishers,
Felinfach, Lampeter,
Dyfed, SA48 8PJ.